# LIVING WATERS

## A Flow of
## *Encouragement* for

## The High School Graduate

## S.D. Horton

A Flow of Encouragement For
# The High School Graduate

Copyright © 2026 by S.D. Horton
ISBN: 978-0-692-28417-9
Cover design by Shannen Palmore
Editorial assistance by Cheryl Horton

Published by

ENTERPRISES

# Contents

## *Dedication*

I dedicate all of my writings to my beautiful wife, Cheryl, who has always supported me and has been one of the main reasons why I pursue my dreams. To my children DeAundre, Jasmine, & Jalen who have always been my inspiration. To my parents, brothers, and body of Christ family who are always there for me with their support and prayers. A **very** special thanks to my life coach and mentor, Dr. Mikel Brown & his wife Debra, for continuously pushing me into living my dream. Words cannot express how my family and I appreciate the mark you have left on our lives. Thank you so much! And finally, to everyone else who has supported me throughout my whole life. Trust me, I know who you are. Thank you for all you have done.

## *Special Thanks*

Special thanks to the family members and friends who have graduated high school over the years. Your testimonies and achievements have greatly assisted me in writing this book of encouragement.

# *Foreword*

The *Living Waters*: *A Flow of Encouragement* series is designed to provide a continuous flow of encouraging words to those who are in need of a "pick-me-up". Life presents many opportunities to everyone, but it also presents problems, failures, and discouragements. You do not have to go through life aimlessly! *A Flow of Encouragement* is here to show you the light at the end of the tunnel. Regardless of the negatives presented in life, or even opposition from people, you can still be a success.

*S.D. Horton*
*Author*

# *Introduction*

Alas, your high school years are over! What's next? Are you afraid of what the future holds for your life? If so, you are not alone. A lot of graduates are nervous about entering into a dimension of life they have never experienced. Many of you have never had a job, never owned a car, or never been away from your home state. To step out into the unknown would be a big step for you.

There's no need to worry. I have great news for you! There is H.O.P.E.! In the following chapters, I will show you how you will always have help, how opportunity will always avail itself to you, how persistence is the key to success, and how endurance will outlast persecution.

# 1

# HELP

Grad Tip

*Seeking help from a large number of people is not always wise.*

# 1

# HELP

**H**elp is always available!  There are many people who have been down the same road you are about to travel on.  Never be afraid to ask people for guidance and direction.  You should always have someone in your life to encourage and strengthen you.  When times get hard (and they will), that person will be there for you through thick and thin.  You can refer to that person as your life coach.  You must be willing to take advice from your life coach.  Remember, the coach has already been where you are trying to go!

WARNING:  Help will try to come in many packages.  Do not be fooled!  Seeking help from a large number of people is not always wise.  You must have one or maybe two people who you designate as helpers for your life.  These individuals must be qualified to speak into your life.  You may ask, "What are the qualifications I must look for?"  Well, one of the first things to look for is integrity.  Be very careful.  There are many people who profess to have integrity, but over a small length of time, their loose tongue tells on them!

## The Integrity Factor

Integrity is a very important attribute to look for in a person.  You need someone who is going to stand for truth with you.  Even when your vision is clouded or you're just simply avoiding the truth;

people of integrity will always tell you the truth even when you don't want to hear it. On the other hand, "flaky" people will tell you things that may only benefit them. They may be with you one moment, but when times get hard, they're criticizing you! You don't need unauthorized people in your circle to drag you down with them in the despair of life. That's why you must be strategic in choosing who will help you. People may mean well, but due to lack of integrity, they are just not for you!

## Self-worth = confidence

Another attribute to look for in a person is self-worth. Believe it or not, if people do not have a healthy self-esteem about themselves, then they won't genuinely care a hill of beans about you. You don't need complainers in your life. As my life coach once told me, complainers are 'crap' magnets. In other words, they attract mess and garbage...things that are not healthy for your life. If you desire to be successful, surround yourself with people who are positive and outgoing. Encircle your life with people who are concerned about how they carry themselves. The confidence protruding from their lives should propel you into greatness and keep you from going through unnecessary steps in life. You are not a 'crap' magnet...you are a success magnet!

## Excellence in all you do

Third, people who thrive for excellence are good people to have in your life. You need people who are going where you're going. If they're not willing to do what it takes to excel, don't waste your time with them. You need people who have a stick-to-itness about themselves...people who are not fickle when trouble arises. Generally, people allow their environment to dictate how they carry themselves in life, and therefore settle in mediocrity. However, people who thrive for excellence dictate their own environment!

3

They control what happens around them. They even control who they allow to be around them. Naturally, you would prefer to utilize a clean restroom in comparison to an un-kept one. Likewise, you should prefer your environment to be clean and conducive to excellence. When people see you, they see someone who's concerned about excelling in life!

# 2

# OPPORTUNITY

Grad Tip

*Opportunity is always knocking at your door.*

# 2

# OPPORTUNITY

Opportunity is always knocking at your door. Whether you choose to continue your education in college or join the military, opportunity will always avail itself to you. But you must discipline yourself! The college life does not have room for students who do not want to do their part (i.e. studying, completing their homework, attending class, etc.) Physically being away from familiar people such as your parents, siblings, and friends can possibly cause you to be lazy. You must train yourself to stay the course, no matter what it takes.

Opportunity is not the only thing knocking at your door. You must be aware of the constant knocking of failure! If you choose to open the door to failure, you will regret it. Failure is not concerned with your best interest. It wants to kick you while you're down. It wants to tell you that you can't make it or you can't do better. Opportunity, on the other hand, will always encourage you. It will pick you up if you fall. I'm reminded of a scripture in the bible when God set before His people life and death. In the same breath, God told them to choose life that they and their descendants may live. Knowing that prosperity, peace, and comfort come with life, I'd rather choose life (opportunity) rather than death (failure).

Now that you know that opportunity and failure will be knocking at your door, which one are you going to answer to? You may have had a taste what failure is like in school through bad grades, failed relationships, etc. You may have tasted what success is like through good grades, successful relationships, etc. Either way, I'm sure you prefer success as opposed to failure. Hear the constant knocking of opportunity. You definitely won't regret it!

# 3

# PERSISTENCE

## Grad Tip

*Persistence will drive you in the direction of where you desire to go.*

# 3

# PERSISTENCE

**P**ersistence is an important key to success. If you do not possess a persistent attitude in life, life itself will swallow you up! You must have the "I am not giving up" mentality. Consider this: It is easier to give up than it is to stay the course. My life coach is always encouraging me to remain diligent in pursuing my dreams. He never allows me to just sit back and "wait" for my dream to come to fruition. Since he has proven himself to be successful in the business arena, my life coach knows what a persistent attitude produces!

A relentless attitude will propel you into higher heights and deeper depths. A lot of people only realize their potential through their persistence. A team down by 3 runs in the bottom of the 9th inning of a baseball game understands that through persistence, a win is inevitable. I recall in many games where teams have had to score 3 or more runs to stage a comeback. It takes resilience to have confidence while at the same time knowing your team is down by 3 runs with 2 outs. A passive manager will show defeat by throwing in the towel, while a persistent manager will seize the opportunity by using pinch hitters, pinch runners, and everything else available in his arsenal to win the game.

Persistence will drive you in the direction of where you desire to go. My life coach encouraged me to find out the price of my dream car, write down the specifications of my dream house, and really push my business so that it will be a success. What was he doing? He was pushing me into persistence! He was encouraging me to be determined enough to achieve my goals. I now understand the rewards of persistence. I understand that it takes tenacity to take what's not going to be handed to you from life.

While working for a particular company, I can recall looking for another job with better benefits, more pay, and more flexibility. The first thing I did was recall what my life coach had been teaching me up to that point. I began to put into practice the things he poured into me. It became a reality when I believed it and spoke it out of my mouth. Now, all I needed was persistence. So I began to do research about the job. I also developed a relationship with the person who was, at that time, in charge of the company I desired to work for. While doing this, I continued to tell my friends about how I believed that the job was already mine. A couple of months later, I started working at my new job! It didn't become a reality when I started working. It became a reality at the moment I believed it and spoke it out of my mouth. Persistence and desire drove me towards it.

# 4

# ENDURANCE

Grad Tip

*Only those with endurance will achieve that which is destined for them to have.*

# 4

# ENDURANCE

Endurance is not for the weak in heart! If you have ever played sports, you have realized that the athlete who comes out on top is always the one who has shown the most endurance. You should always be the one who wants to take the winning shot in a basketball game or catch the winning touchdown in a football game. It takes endurance to get to that point. No matter how tired you are, endurance takes over! When the coach calls your number, fatigue is not a factor because you have trained your body to endure, although your muscles are exhausted. Be ready to stand in the fight! Life does not give handouts! You must come to the mindset that you're going to do whatever it takes to get the prize you are going after!

You are not in high school anymore. You don't have the luxury of depending on your school teachers to bail you out any longer. Your classmates are not there for you anymore. They can't help you with the test you're now about to experience. You must learn how to endure. You must learn to take the blows from life and keep going. Remember, life is not going to hand you anything. Only those with endurance will achieve that which is destined for them to have. Don't be like the ones who settle for the small things. Be different and think bigger! Be one who is always achieving something. Be someone who will always be looked at as a person who conquers anything presented to you. My life coach told me that endurance always outlasts persecution. What a true and profound statement! Sometimes it may seem like you're the only one believing in yourself. At that time, you must still endure. Even when you know for a surety that people want you to fail, you still must endure! Persecution is only a speed bump in life designed to steer you off course. Your desire to carry on, however, is what drives you through the persecutions and pitfalls in life.

Now you are on your own. Go out there and fight for what you have the right to possess! If you fall, get up immediately and go at it again. If you are doing the same thing and getting the same negative results, do not give up! Just change your strategy. Do not settle for the norm. You are your greatest asset. You have a lot to offer to the world. Open up and let your gifts and talents flow out of you like a waterfall!

# *Conclusion*

Congratulations high school graduate! You have entered into a session of life that's going to require hard work and dedication. Remember, you are destined to succeed! Don't allow anyone or anything keep you from being the best you can be!

## *About the Author*

S.D. Horton is a successful businessman, author, and religious leader in a local church. He was born in Columbus, GA and raised in Talbotton, GA. He is an Air Force veteran and currently resides in Alamogordo, NM with his wife.

www.ingramcontent.com/pod-product-compliance
Lightning Source LLC
Chambersburg PA
CBHW070951040426
42443CB00012B/3302